Death and Judgement

Also by Dom Anscar Vonier
Published by Assumption Press

Death and Judgement

Dom Anscar Vonier

Abbot of Buckfast

2013

✠ Nihil Obstat.
Arthur J. Scanlon S.T.D.,
Censor Librorum.

✠ Imprimatur.
Patrick Cardinal Hayes
Archbishop.

New York
March 5, 1931

The *Nihil Obstat* and *Imprimatur* are official declarations
that a book or pamphlet is free of doctrinal or moral error.
No implication is contained therein that those who have
granted the *Nihil Obstat* and the *Imprimatur* agree
with the content, opinions or statements expressed.

This book was originally published in 1931
by the MacMillan Coompany.

Cover image: *The Last Judgement,* Hans Memling, c. 1467-71

CONTENTS

I

THE CAUSE OF DEATH

Death has with man far-reaching philosophical and theological implications. We may grant to the physiologist all he wants and all he claims; he is no enemy of the Christian faith so long as he remains within his own province of physiological and material happenings. We may leave it to him to explain to us how death occurs. No doubt scientists find it as hard to define death in terms of biology as theologians and philosophers find it difficult to give an answer to all the queries that are raised by the materialist and the unbeliever. As an instance of such an attempt on the part of science to state the causes of death in terms which have some meaning, I may quote from the *Encyclopaedia Britannica*, under the word Biology:

> Recent investigations point to the conclusion that the immediate cause of the arrest of vitality, in the first place, and of its destruction, in the second, is the coagulation of certain substances in the protoplasm, and that the lat-

ter contains various coagulable matters, which solidify at
different temperatures. And it remains to be seen, how
far the death of any form of living matter, at a given tem-
perature, depends on the destruction of its fundamental
substance at that heat, and how far death is brought about
by the coagulation of merely accessory compounds.

From this passage we see the hesitation of even the most
recent investigators when they try to define death otherwise
than by the accidental signs which show that it has occurred.
Catholic theologians and philosophers will welcome further
elucidation of the causes of this terrible phenomenon.

As Christians we have our own problems on the matter
of death, one of which may be assigned to the theologian
and one to the philosopher. The theologian inquires why
it is that mankind in general regards death as a penal arrangement. The philosopher's question is different: he asks
how the phenomenon can take place in spite of the spiritual
soul.

Catholic faith, which is the proper province of the theologian, teaches that the death of man is a punishment:

By one man sin entered into this world and by sin death;
and so death passed upon all men (Rom 5:12).

Catholic faith does not consider the death of animals
to be in any way or in any sense penal, but of man's death
it deliberately says that it is the result of sin. How did such
a reading of the phenomenon of death originate? Why is it
considered to be a punitive measure, when to all appearanc-
es it has the inevitableness of a similar law of nature to that

which governs the death of animals? How can an event in the natural order be turned into a castigation? The answer is found in the potency of a presupposition. Faith presupposes something of which it alone can have knowledge: it presupposes that God made the bodily frame of man immortal by means of a special gift, a gift added to human nature, even detachable from it. God intended all mankind to possess this extra gift—the gift of immortality. Man lost it through his sin, through his own guilty act. So—always in the presupposition of this additional gift—it is perfectly accurate to say that death is a punishment, not a normal occurrence.

Theologians commonly admit that without that gift man is not, indeed could not be, immortal in his body. We do not pretend to know or say that it would not be possible for the Creator to make a living bodily organism which could endure for ever in virtue of its own intrinsic natural constituents. Most likely it is not beyond the power of the Creator to produce such an organism; theology is not concerned with such an hypothesis. Our speculations must be confined to that organism of which we have experience and of which it is said in the Book of Genesis that it was formed from the slime of the earth. Of such an organism theology says that, though left to itself it must sooner or later decay, such decay was not according to God's first intentions, but that he planned to prevent that decay by an additional gift of an entirely supernatural character. The forfeiture of this gift through the act of sin may be truly considered as the cause of death in this relative sense of a presupposition. It would be rash to deny to God the power to make a bodily organism which should be *naturally* immortal. Had he so made man, sin would not have had death for its penalty, since God never destroys that which is according to nature. Such, however, were not the ways of God in the creation of man. He did not make man naturally immortal in his bodily frame; on the contrary, he made him naturally mortal, but he added to mortality the gift of supernatural immortality. Now that which is supernatural—except, of course, the state of Beatific Vision—can always be lost or forfeited. That terrific insistence of God on man's fundamental mortality is the key to the chapter of the Fall in Genesis:

> In the sweat of thy face shalt thou eat bread till thou return to the earth, out of which thou wert taken: for dust thou art, and into dust thou shalt return (Gen 3:19).

The gift of immortality conferred by God on man was entirely gratuitous and supernatural in quality. In what it really consisted it is impossible for us to say or even to imagine. It was more than an external watchfulness, guarding man from all possible forces that might have caused death; it was an inherent and intrinsic quality, though one that could be lost, as grace also could be lost. It was in man's power to live, but it was also in his power to die, if he chose to prove faithless to God's pact with him:

> Of the tree of knowledge of good and evil, thou shalt not eat. For in what day soever thou shalt eat of it, thou shalt die the death (Gen 2:17).

Death, then, was known to man as a possible contingency even in the days of his innocence. Adam did not know evil; he did not know that he was naked; but he did know, even then when he was in that state of blissful ignorance, that he could die; the meaning of the word death was clear to him:

> Of the fruit of the tree which is in the midst of paradise, God hath commanded us that we should not touch it, lest perhaps we die. And the serpent said to the woman: No, you shall not die the death (Gen 3:3-4).

This clear appreciation of the meaning of death by man, when as yet he knew no evil, brings out most strongly the gratuitous, one might almost say the precarious, nature of the gift of possible immortality which had been bestowed on him.

It is therefore evident that the Catholic tradition which considers death as a penal arrangement in no wise interferes with the investigations of the physiologist into the causes of death. Is it not the very essence of Catholic thought in this matter to assume that man's punishment lies in this particular thing, that his body should be left to its congenital weakness, to its natural decay, when the arresting or healing supernatural quality of immortality is gone? Let us sum up these considerations in the concise words of St Thomas:

> Death is natural on account of the conditions of matter, but it is penal on account of the loss of the divine gift which has power to preserve from death (*Summa* II-II, q. 164, a 1).

But the theologian is not the only authority to be assailed by the exclusively secular explanation of death. The Catholic philosopher, and especially the scholastic philosopher, is called upon to explain how, with the doctrine which he holds concerning the human soul, he can pretend to leave death to merely physiological causalities. If a spiritual essence, an immortal soul, animates the body, if it is, in scholastic terminology, the *forma* of the body, is it not to be assumed that death occurs then only—can occur then only—when that soul departs from the body? For, since the soul is supposed to be the very principle and source of life to the body, so long as it is in the body the physical organism must be alive. Now, says the physiologist, the phenomenon of death belongs entirely to the material realm of things; at no time, at no stage of bodily decadence is anything either arrested or modified by some mystical agency called the "soul." It has not been found necessary to define death as the departure of the soul; death is sufficiently explained and amply described, says not only the materialist but even the vitalist, through causes which do not transcend the order of observable data. The physiologist is, of course, quite right in his contention as to the physical nature of the factors that bring about death in man; but he is wrong in supposing, as he constantly does, at least by implication, that if there really were an immortal soul in man things would take a different course. The innuendo is, obviously, that there is no soul at all; with a soul man could not die, such is the unspoken conclusion of the adversary of spiritualistic philosophy.

It is, however, the very nature of the soul's abiding presence in man to be of such a kind that the phenomenon of death is not meant to be arrested by the soul at any time or under any circumstances, nor to be interfered with by it; Catholic philosophy has never regarded the soul as having any such office or function. We may say that the presence of an immortal soul in man may be viewed either loosely or strictly, according to the school to which Christian thinkers belong. The looser view is more imaginative, more phenomenalist; it looks upon the spiritual soul as upon an extramundane substance dwelling in a material body. To those thinkers or rather philosophical poets who hold such views death would be the destruction of the house of the soul, a destruction brought about by quite material agencies. The house being destroyed, the soul takes to its wings, goes forth into the world of pure spirits, either good or bad. Such poetry would be sufficient to visualize death as being a fact entirely of this earth.

The task of the strict scholastic, who is also the more exact Catholic thinker, will, however, be more difficult. For him the spiritual soul in man is the "form" of the body, the principle of oneness in man's life and personality. The soul, in orthodox Catholic philosophy, is much more than a dweller in the body; it is to the body the cause of much that makes of it what it is. Can the scholastic, who is also a Catholic, serenely ignore the soul in the phenomenon of death, when his whole philosophy makes him hold that the union between soul and body in man is the greatest and most intimate of all partnerships? The answer is that the schoolmen, like the modern physiologists, look to entirely material agencies as the causes of death in man. For the scholastic, death is not a separation between soul and body; it is the breaking up, the "dissolution" of the body. The soul is said to depart because death has occurred, because the organism has died, not *vice versa*: man is not dead because the soul has left the body, but because he is dead the soul departs.

All this is in conformity with that special mode of function which our philosophy attributes to the soul. The soul is to the body a formal cause, not an efficient cause: this distinction is the root of that important piece of created reality. A spirit like the soul can only be the "form" of a body if certain material dispositions and predispositions are provided for its reception. These all-important predispositions are produced by efficient causes, the generating parent, and many other factors. Now, other efficient causes may undermine those indispensable dispositions, nay even destroy them completely. This is the action we call death. The dispositions gone, the soul can no more be "form" to the body: the very definition of "form" would be against any such continuance.

We are not here concerned with the survival of the soul after death nor the soul's fate and future when it ceases to "inform" the body; these are points to be treated fully by and by. Our task now is to make clear that, according to the very tenets of our spiritualistic philosophy, our belief in the presence of a soul in man does not compel us to explain death otherwise than by a chain of causes which are exclusively of the material order.

II

DEATH AND THE SUPERNATURAL ORDER

If in our first chapter we have conceded all that is needful to the modern views concerning the natural and material explanation of the phenomenon of death in man, we do not on this account deprive death of all supernatural and spiritual significance. Though it be the result of forces that are not by any manner of means mystical, death is a most mystical factor in the economy of man's ultimate sanctification and salvation. According to Catholic theology, death has a threefold action on the whole scheme of final election: its occurrence is part of man's predestination; its universality is part of man's satisfaction to divine Justice; its wholesale destructiveness puts an end to man's power of meriting, and places him in the *status termini*, the condition of finality, with regard to his spiritual state. God has kept this instrument of severity in his own hands, and uses it for the purposes of his mercy and justice, not only in a general way, but in relation to individual human beings.

We need not enter into all the profundities of the Catholic doctrine of predestination. It is orthodox to confess that all those who are saved are brought into the harbor of eternal life through a direct act of God, whilst it is heresy to say that those who are lost are predestinated by God to so terrible a fate. Catholic theology upholds most energetically the necessity of predestination, but it knows of no predestination that is not for heaven. To bring about this end God multiplies graces and shapes the external settings of the individual human lives of the elect. The *opportunitas mortis*, the propitious moment of death, is the principal of those outward arrangements of the predestinating Providence, man being taken away from this earth, which is the place of temptation and of crisis, at a time when he is in the friendship of God, when he is fit for heaven. It is possible for God to bestow on a human being the gift of impeccability. Our Lady possessed it; so also did the Apostles, in the sense that after the descent of the Holy Ghost they could never more sin grievously. Such people are said to be confirmed in grace, not through an inherent gift, but through the fact that, through the providence of God, death overtakes them in a state of grace. Such an opportuneness of death is a part of the positive ordinance of God to secure the ultimate salvation of the soul:

> But the just man, if he be prevented with death, shall
> be in rest. For venerable old age is not that of long time,
> nor counted by the number of years: but the understand-
> ing of a man is grey hairs. And a spotless life is old age
> (Wis 4:7-9).

Unless a man be endowed with the supreme gift of confirmation in grace, at no time of his life is his virtue such that it could not fail under the stress of temptation; it is always an act of God's merciful disposition if he sends death at the time when a man is in a state of grace. Quite technically, the great Spanish theologian, Joannes a St. Thoma, puts the matter thus:

> If we consider death as the indispensable condition for acquiring fixity in the state of grace and for being admitted to heavenly glory, death thus viewed is a gift of God's especial providence. ... The special gift of death may be called an exceptional favor of an external nature because it means a very particular protection on the part of God against temptation and against those obstacles which stand in the way of eternal glory, lest they arise or lest they overcome man if they do arise (*De Gratia,* Disp. 21, a. 2).

The second supernatural aspect of death, the satisfaction of divine Justice, opens out a vast theological field. We can only lay down here the fundamental principle of satisfaction by human death in its widest outlines. We must make clear distinction between death and those ills, more or less consciously felt by men, which in most cases precede death and are its forerunners. What we say on death in this book is to be understood to bear exclusively on the cessation of life; whether that cessation be painful or not does not affect our speculation. The laying down of life, the return of man to the dust from which he was taken, this is death, with all its theological implications. Now this is, in God's supernatural province, a complete atonement for all sin, provided we include in the cycle of human death the death of the God-Man Jesus Christ, as it should be included.

It is a universal proposition, which for Christians is unassailable, that death has satisfied for man's sin. No other human happening has this effect to the same extent. The relationship which exists between the death of ordinary human beings in their countless millions and the death of the Son of God will be seen in another place; but we may consider at once the extent to which the death of every individual man is a power of satisfaction for sin. That it is the normal, the most efficacious mode of paying to God what is technically called the "debt of temporal punishment" is evident from the very words in which God announced to Adam the results of his sin. Above all we must consider the death of the Christian who willingly and consciously accepts the chastisement in union with Christ's death, to be the most potent cleansing of man's soul. There is, of course, more; there is in death a possibility of justice and sanctification which goes beyond its penal character. Man may die for justice' sake, as a martyr for Christ, as a witness to the Faith of Christ. Now "martyrdom must include death": *Mors est de ratione martyrii* (*Summa* II-II, q. 124, a. 4).

In martyrdom death as death is the glory, quite apart from the many virtues that may have preceded it while the martyr languished in his torments. To have died for the Faith of Christ is the supreme ennobling of human death, is its highest supernatural role in the merely human sphere.

The third connection which death has with supernatural life is of a less positive character than the two preceding ones, though its theological importance is truly unfathomable. Through death there comes a sudden and permanent standstill to that mighty forward movement of man's soul which had been produced by the grace of God. The period of spiritual change, of merit, of progress, is forever at an end. Henceforth there can be manifestation of the life that is in man through grace, but there can be no further advance on the road of sanctity; death destroys in man the very capacity to change, to progress, to rise higher. This "power of meriting," as it is technically called, vanishes at death as completely as life itself.

We do not consider at this stage that state of fixity of purpose in which the soul of man finds itself through its separation from the body at death; that is a separate factor, and will be dealt with in this book in due course. At death man's soul becomes unchangeable. But this is not the reason of that tremendous halt in his spiritual life which Catholic faith associates with death. Man ceases to merit, to gain fresh rewards, because death destroys in him all his true human working powers. All the supernatural store of merit must be acquired by deeds done in the body; we know of no virtue that is not a deed done in the body, however sublime and mystical that virtue may be:

> You have not chosen me: but I have chosen you; and
> have appointed you, that you should go and bring forth
> fruit; and your fruit should remain; that whatsoever you
> shall ask of the Father in my name, he may give it you
> (John 15:16).

The fruitfulness referred to in the text is to take place on this earth; there will be no fruitfulness hereafter, only the gathering of the fruits. This cessation of merit at death is an essential doctrine in the Catholic view of man's justification and salvation. Innumerable authorities could be quoted to show the persevering conviction of the Church that the present life is man's only chance for doing the works that will be rewarded with increased heavenly bliss:

> "I must work the works of him that sent me, whilst it is day: the night cometh, when no man can work (John 9:4).

In these words Christ undoubtedly states that very far-reaching truth. Christianity would indeed be quite incomprehensible if we did not take the bodily death of man for an absolute and final limit of his spiritual possibilities. The great systematizer of practical spiritual life in the sixth century, St Benedict, voices the mind of the Church in his own period, a period of great maturity in the Christian conscience:

> If we would arrive at eternal life, escaping the pains of hell, then—while there is yet time, while we are still in the flesh, and are able to fulfill all these things by the light which is now given us—we must hasten to do what will profit us for all eternity (Prologue, *Holy Rule*).

It would be difficult to give the ultimate reason why, in the dispensation of God's grace, death has become this impassable limit. Is it a positive ordinance or is it in the very nature of things? It is certain that at death man ceases to be truly man; though his spirit survive, he cannot do the deeds of man anymore, so it would seem that it becomes inevitable for merit and progress to be then brought to a standstill. The glories that come to a soul when it enters heaven, the splendors of the risen body on the day of the general Resurrection, will not be new things, they will merely be the manifestation of the perfections that were in us when we lived and died in the supernatural state:

> Dearly beloved, we are now the sons of God: and it hath not yet appeared what we shall be. We know that when he shall appear we shall be like to him: because we shall see him as he is (1 John 3:2).

III

THE PROVISIONAL NATURE OF DEATH

Nothing is more certain in Christian faith than the provisional nature of death. However dimly the saints of the Old Law may have apprehended this truth, with the Resurrection of Christ from the dead the idea that death is not final but only provisional established itself with unconquerable splendor of certainty. In the words of St Paul, Jesus Christ "hath destroyed death and hath brought to light life and incorruption" (2 Tim 1:10). Death, in the phraseology of the New Testament, is considered as an enemy to be conquered by God. Death is personified, not only in the Apocalypse of St John but also in the writings of the Apostles, very much as it was represented in all medieval literature and art. Now this grim tyrant must be overcome completely if the work of God is to be a success at all.

We may here make a distinction between the doctrine of the Resurrection and that other truth, the destruction of death and its ultimate defeat. It may be said that the Christian belief in God's final victory over death is a larger and more comprehensive faith than the belief in the Resurrection, because the raising up of the dead might be followed, at least hypothetically, by another death, whilst that triumph over death of which the New Testament speaks is a complete abolition of death for all times, under all circumstances, both for the good and for the wicked. That such is Christian doctrine is beyond all question, and it is important in our days to lay stress on this ancient dogma of the Church. Today more than ever men preach a restoration of things in Christ which does not contain the destruction of death; they even speak of Resurrection in the Person of Christ and also for the human race, in terms which are not truly expressive of a victory of God over death. Man, they say, is given a new life. Out of death new existences are born; the spirit triumphs over death in the sense that it survives death, it mocks death, it eludes death in a mystical triumph, but death, as death, is not overcome. Now, this is not Christianity. Unless we profess that God will one day abolish that very order of things which he established when he said to man: "Thou shalt die the death" (Gen 2:17), we have not grasped the full power of Christ's Redemption.

Catholic thought is all in favor of the blissful state of the souls of the elect during that period of expectation which precedes the resurrection of the flesh; in fact, we are so used to the spiritual intercourse with the saints as they are now in the state of disembodiment that it is one of the tasks of the accurate theologian to remind the Christian people that the present state of the elect, however blissful, is by no means that state of glorious consummation towards which all things are working in the great dispensation of the mystery of Christ. We are inclined, more or less consciously, to endow the spirits of the saints with that condition of complete human personality which will only be real and actual after the Resurrection. But, even if the spiritual prerogatives of the elect in their disembodied existence were greater than they are, it is certain that such bliss is by no means and in no sense that victory over death which is Christ's own particular triumph and glory. By way of a bold hypothesis, let us suppose that those elect were given a bodily frame by God's omnipotence, entirely disconnected with anything they ever possessed in their mortal days, such a completion of their personalities would not be that triumph over death which is Christ's supreme act and the final evidence of his possession of all power. The words of our Scriptures are so telling that nothing but a complete reversal of those conditions which exist since man's fall will do them justice. Death is cancelled by Christ. Death is swallowed up by Christ:

> Who is on the right hand of God, swallowing down death that we might be made heirs of life everlasting (1 Pet 3:22).

Death is wiped out, as sin is wiped out, by Christ. The human race, through the power of Christ as its Redeemer, will be a race of beings that were dead and live again for ever and ever, even as Christ was dead and lives for ever and ever, as if death had never touched them, so complete is Christ's mastery over death.

It is Christian faith to admit that not the elect only will rise from the dead but the whole human race, good and bad:

> The hour cometh, wherein all that are in the graves
> shall hear the voice of the Son of God (John 5:28).

The resurrection of the elect and their immortality presents
no special difficulties, as we can readily grant to Christ the
power of pouring out gifts of life of the supernatural kind
on those blessed ones who share his life. But how shall we
explain the immortality of the reprobate? Here, of course,
we cannot give as an explanation the bestowal upon them
of supernatural vitalities, as, by very definition, they are excluded from all such vitalities. At this point we see the necessity of a dogma vaster than the dogma of the supernatural resurrection in Christ; we need the dogma of Christ's
universal victory over death, not only in the supernatural
but even in the natural order. How mankind, universally
speaking, prescinding from the supernatural and the natural
order, will be rendered inaccessible forever to death, need
not be explained here. The new world which God will make
out of the old will have properties and qualities, even on the
material side, not known to this present order of things.

IV

The Death of the Son of God

It would be a grave omission in our speculations on death if we did not pay a good deal of attention to the mystery of the death of Jesus Christ, the Son of God. The fact that the God Incarnate died so deeply affects the Christian theology on death that one might almost say that to the Christian death has an entirely different meaning from its significance in exclusively pagan thought. It is, of course, evident that the event of Christ's death on the Cross can be studied, and indeed, must be studied, from many different angles. Above all, that great death is the supreme ritual sacrifice of the New Covenant, but nothing is more certain in Catholic theology than the reaction of all the happenings of Christ's career on similar happenings in the careers of ordinary human beings. Thus all the virtuous deeds of the God-Man whilst here on earth have a direct influence on our own acts of virtue, and we must take it for granted that the death of man is immediately affected, in some very true though mysterious fashion, by the death of the Son of God. If God himself died, if God at one time was amongst the dead, death cannot any longer be an unmitigated evil: to be dead cannot be a desperate and hopeless condition: to die cannot be any more a matter of real terror:

> Therefore because the children are partakers of flesh and blood, he also himself in like manner hath been partaker of the same: that, through death, he might destroy him who had the empire of death, that is to say, the devil: And might deliver them who through the fear of death were all their lifetime subject to servitude (Heb 2:14-15).

There is, as we know, in the death of Christ that supreme value of satisfaction to the justice of God through which we have confidence in God at all times, in life and in death; but there is also in the death of Christ the aspect of exemplariness in a high degree: Christ died in order to share that universal human condition, and to give that condition the supporting splendour of his personality. So it is an ever-recurring thought in New Testament theology that between life and death there is no longer any real chasm, because Christ, having tasted of both conditions, life and death, has bridged the abyss between the two:

> For none of us liveth to himself: and no man dieth to himself. For whether we live, we live unto the Lord: or whether we die, we die unto the Lord. Therefore, whether we live or whether we die, we are the Lord's. For to this end Christ died and rose again: that he might be the Lord both of the dead and of the living (Rom 14:7-9).

Life and death are equally profitable to the Christian:

> For all things are yours ... the world, or life, or things present, or things to come (1 Cor 3:22).

The devotion of the Christian people to Christ in his death is one of the soundest and deepest manifestations of the genius of our spirit: to glory in the death of Christ is the source of Christian joyfulness:

> Together, death and life in a strange conflict strove. The Prince of life, who died, now lives and reigns (Easter Sequence).

The Church in her liturgy never grows tired of those ideas that through death we have life, that in death we are vivified, that the death of God is man's birth. Death is no longer something catastrophic, but, through Christ, has become one of the functions of our supernatural life in the Son of God; it is good for us to die, even as Christ has died:

> For God hath not appointed us unto wrath: but unto the purchasing of salvation by our Lord Jesus Christ, who died for us: that, whether we watch or sleep, we may live together with him. For which cause comfort one another and edify one another, as you also do (1 Thess. 5:9-11).

We ought not to omit here certain considerations which belong more directly to a treatise on the Incarnation, but whose connexion with the present matter is evident. Though Catholic theology upholds the exemplariness of Christ's death and considers it as a pivotal thought in Christian mentality, it is also the concern of that same Catholic theology to bring out the differences between the death of

Christ and the decease of all other human beings. That there are profound differences is evident. The one thing certain in Christ's death is this, that his Spirit, his Soul, left the Body:

> Being put to death indeed in the flesh, but enlivened in the spirit (1 Pet 3:18).

Perhaps we may say that Christ's is the only death which consists precisely in this, that the soul was separated from the body. We know for certain that the divine Nature was not separated from Christ's Body at death. The Body which Joseph of Arimathea and Nicodemus laid in the tomb remained as much the temple of the Godhead, remained as completely and as immediately united hypostatically with the Second Person of the Trinity as it had been during life. Moreover, we know that this most holy Body never saw corruption, the process of organic disintegration is no part of the death of Christ. For this reason and others the doctors of the Church have always looked upon Christ's death as one of the marvels of the Incarnation; they have never fallen victim to the temptation of heaping up indignities in order to make the stupendous sacrifice even more impressive to the imagination.

V

MAN'S SOUL AT DEATH

It has become the ineradicable fashion of philosophical writers to apply the term immortality, not to man's bodily organism, but to his soul. Of the soul it is asked whether it be mortal or immortal, and in modern phraseology the whole question of man's immortality centres round the hotly debated point whether the human soul survives the disintegration of the body, or if there be no such survival. That the paramount doctrine of immortality in Christian thought is primarily concerned with the whole man, with man in his bodily frame as well as in his spiritual elements, seems to be an idea which has been dislodged from the contemporary intellect for ever. The revelations in the New Testament concerning immortality are, as we have seen, invariably expressions of the vaster faith, man's total restoration in Christ; the soul's survival is hinted at, but St. Paul's inspired enthusiasms about our future state reveal without exception the sense of victory over bodily death through the resurrection of the flesh.

With this overwhelming mode of expression in modern philosophical and theological literature, it becomes inevitable that the great problem of the survival of man's soul should be described as the problem of the soul's immortality; but it would be sufficient, and vastly more logical, to speak of the soul's spirituality. If it be admitted that man's soul is a truly spiritual substance, with no material elements in its composition, then its imperviability to death, its so-called immortality, is for ever established. No man in his senses would for one moment hesitate to admit such a conclusion. Death makes no difference to the soul's real status, it becomes neither more spiritual nor more imperishable than it is during man's lifetime; it remains what it has always been—an unmixed spiritual substance. So the problem of the soul's immortality and survival should not be deferred to the moment of death; the consideration should be formulated and discussed at every stage of man's career, at his birth, at the maturity of his conscious powers, at the period of his decadence. Is there or is there not in man a spiritual substance called "soul" which is superior to all sense-life? If this mighty query be answered in the affirmative, then we have the soul's immortality, even were we to take a child's conscious life as the field of our philosophical investigation. The only new problem which death would present is the mystery of the soul's abode, as we might call it, when the bodily habitation which it enjoyed has become the howling wilderness of disintegration. Although the great problem of the soul's immortality is not first raised on account of death, but is only rendered more acute thereby, it is natural for man, when he sees human personality thus brought to nought, to ask himself with increased insistence and anxiety whether there is anything in man that does endure for ever, whether he may in truth say of himself *non totus moriar.* Thus from this point of view the soul's survival becomes more particularly associated with death, though the reasons on which Christian doctrine bases the possibility of such survival are reasons which hold good through every period and condition of man's life. The only ground on which we can establish the principle that the soul cannot die is this, that it is spiritual and that it has always been spiritual; it is not death-proof through some hidden, extrinsic quality which only asserts itself at the demolition of the body.

The evidences which establish the doctrine that in man there is a truly spiritual substance, united with the body though independent of it, are, in the last analysis easily classed under three headings. There is first the whole attitude of the Christian Church, which assumes a spiritual soul in man. Secondly, there is the natural, historic tradition of mankind. Then, in the third place, we have the findings and conclusions of spiritualistic philosophy, from the Greeks down to our own days.

I call the Church's testimony in this matter an attitude. The fact is that Catholicism, in its whole presentment of spiritual life as the outpouring of the Holy Ghost, postulates in man a spirit that is the fit recipient of the graces of the Paraclete, of the regenerative power of the Sacraments, of the mystical union with Christ. The practical view which the Church takes of man, the whole man, is such that unless there be in him a higher thing than flesh and blood the Church's ministry would be meaningless.

Little is said, either in the Old or the New Testament, of the soul of man in sharp contradistinction to the body, as is so largely done in the non-inspired and more modern religious literature. As already said, Christianity has founded its own hopes of immortality on Christ's victory over death, and it has never thought it necessary to explain the soul's immortality with a kind of feverish insistence, in order to strengthen the belief of Christians in an eternal life. But life in Christ as propounded by Christianity is such that it demands at all times in man that image and likeness of God which is the spiritual soul.

Mankind has always believed in a spirit in man, a spirit that could withdraw from the body at death. But since it is of less interest to men to know that there is in them a spiritual soul while they enjoy the good things of life than it is to be assured that at death all their chances of existence have not come to an end, this unreasoned faith has certainly been more pronounced with regard to the dead than with regard to the living. Thus on most men this great philosophical and religious matter presses more urgently in connexion with death rather than during life. All this implies that the immense majority of human beings always have held the conviction that in man there was a spirit which would go forth from him at the moment of his bodily decease.

The findings of rational psychology are varied in mode of approach, but they are at one in the centre. The activities of man during life are of a kind that presupposes in him a principle which transcends matter, sense, space and time. Whatever we may call this tremendous force, whether a sense of duty, a desire of immortality, a love of beauty or universality of thought, it is always one and the same mysterious reality: an activity in man which is not limited by sense-life. Therefore the principle of such activity, the soul, is ultimately beyond the senses. But I must not pursue this line of thought further; if fully followed up volumes might be written upon it.

Wonder has been expressed very often that throughout the Old Testament there is almost complete silence on the subject of man's soul and on the fate of that soul at death. Critics have gone so far as to accuse the writers of the Old Testament of materialism, of lack of faith in a Hereafter. But the same reproach might be formulated against the New Testament also; special and express mention of the soul is not easy to find either in the Gospels or the Epistles; man himself is always the theme of the inspired writers.

Now there is nothing clearer than the view which the two Testaments take of man. Either individually or as a nation, man is essentially a being with definite moral responsibilities, and those responsibilities are of the highest kind, at all times. God enters into judgement with man has clear relationships with him, both in his social and individual status. Herein may lie a difference between the Old and the New Testaments, that the ancient writers and prophets were more concerned with mankind as a nation, while in the New Testament greater allowance is made for man, individually. But even this distinction must not be pressed, as the corporate life of the Christians is not less pronounced than the corporate life of the Jewish race, that perennial bride of God. Should we not see in this very uniformity of thought in the inspired writers a mark of their supreme grasp of man's true nature and mission? It would certainly be an immense loss to our religious literature if the prophets and the apostles had abandoned their vast style of visualising mankind and had sunk to mere solicitude concerning individual souls. Let us always remember that the inspired writers are what they are because they express, not the thoughts of man, but the thoughts of God.

VI

THE STATE OF THE HUMAN SOUL
AFTER DEATH

The survival of man's soul after the disintegration of death once granted, there arises the entrancing but also perplexing subject of the conditions under which that soul exists when thus separated from the body. This grave question, in spite of its obscurity, has always possessed a kind of allurement for the human mind. From the cult of the saints down to necromancy, the powers of the discarnate human spirits have always played a great role in the religious history of mankind. The data of Catholic revelation are clear but few, and they are concerned only with the souls of the elect, the saved. At death, says the Catholic Church, the human soul, if it be in a state of perfect charity, will enter into heavenly bliss, without any retardation. It will enjoy the Vision of God in an entirely intellectual way in a degree that will correspond with the supernatural merits acquired by it during life. The soul will not be in a state of unconsciousness, but will be fully aware of its own existence, its election, its final escape from evil. To a great extent it will be in a state of expectation, awaiting reunion with the body; without which man's life, even his glorified life, cannot be full and entire. In that condition of disembodied happiness the souls of the saved constitute a portion of Christ's Church; they are the Church Triumphant; they are in communion with the Church here on earth, they receive our prayers, they intercede for us before the Throne of God.

If the soul of the Christian, though in a state of grace at death, yet be not perfect in charity, then admission to heavenly bliss is retarded; the soul is perfected through a mysterious process called purgatory. Discarnate spirits in that state are also part of the Church; they are the Suffering Church; they are in communion with the rest of the Church passively, receiving the benefit of the intercession of all other Christians.

All these things have been said excellently in other parts of this series; my task is to make clear the more intimate conditions of the disembodied human soul, conditions which will apply to all souls, irrespective of the supernatural state, irrespective even of happiness and misery.

The question to be settled here, as far as it is possible to do so, is the special psychological state of those spirits of the dead. What is a disembodied human soul? What powers, what consciousness, what knowledge does it possess? In other words, we are trying to find out the natural results of death on the soul itself. In this investigation we have only rational philosophy to guide us; all our conclusions come from the true understanding of the difference between matter and spirit, sense and intellect.

Now such a study has been made with very great care and assiduity by Catholic thinkers, chiefly by the scholastic philosophers; they have left us a body of sound speculation on this abstruse subject which is the last word in the matter, so far, indeed, as man can speak a last word on so high a plane of thought. St. Thomas has quite a preference for the subject and his reasonings on the *Anima separata*—the separated soul—are a great contribution to Catholic speculation. The Scriptures cannot help us in this sphere of abstract consideration; they take for granted the survival of the soul, principally the elect soul; when they speak of it they necessarily give it all the attributes of a complete human personality, ascribing to it a behavior that belongs to the risen state, when body and soul will be reunited:

> And when he had opened the fifth seal, I saw under the altar the souls of them that were slain for the word of God and for the testimony which they held. And they cried with a loud voice, saying: How long, O Lord (Holy and True), dost thou not judge and revenge our blood on them that dwell on the earth? And white robes were given, to every one of them one. And it was said to them that they should rest for a little time till their fellow servants and their brethren, who are to be slain even as they, should be filled up (Rev 6:9-11).

In our liturgical life we do the same thing. We address the saints in heaven, not as discarnate spirits, but as fully constituted human personalities. We could not, under any circumstances, render them present to our thoughts in a disembodied state.

The philosophical principles which have enabled Catholic thinkers to establish the spirituality of the human soul on rational grounds are also the principles which have guided them in laying down clear data concerning the disembodied human spirits. We say that man's soul is entirely spiritual because during life it has entirely spiritual operations. From this St. Thomas concludes, with all other scholastics, that only such portions or powers of man's soul are found in the discarnate state as are entirely spiritual; for the whole scholastic case with regard to the soul's survival turns on that one fact, the complete immateriality of certain acts of man in lifetime. So they arrive at this very rational conclusion that only those things remain after death which are entirely immaterial, without any admixture of matter and sense-life. If the discarnate spirit were supposed still to possess material elements or sense-life, even of the most refined description, there would be no reason, says St. Thomas, why we should not grant immortality also to the souls of animals. If sense-life of any kind could survive death, then the animal soul could survive death; but this hypothesis is an absurdity to Catholic thinkers. So all our philosophical premises postulate this, that only an entirely immaterial substance, with immaterial powers and immaterial operations, can survive death. Consequently the discarnate soul of man is, in the eyes of Catholic philosophers, an exclusively spiritual being; in fact, it is a spirit.

From this we see that Catholic philosophy, whilst upholding the soul's survival, admits that the havoc of death is much greater than less logical thinkers would make it. All that part of the human mind which is concerned with sense-life, even of the highest type, perishes at death. There is in man, truly, the perishable mind as Aristotle already saw it, but there is also in man the imperishable mind, also as Aristotle saw it, I mean the exclusively intellectual mind; that mind remains. Only let us remember that when we speak of the perishable and the imperishable mind we are not speaking of two souls, but of two different powers in the one soul, whose root or substance is entirely spiritual. So the discarnate spirit of man is credited by scholastic philosophy with two powers only, the power of intellection and the power of volition; all other operations, however wonderful, however aesthetic, have been left behind at death, they perish with the body. So our dead are truly for us mysterious beings; we can only think of them by clothing them in our imagination with a humanity which is not theirs any more, but which will be theirs again when death will be overcome by Christ.

The question to ask now is this: what is the extent of that intellectual and volitive life which Catholic philosophy grants to the separated human soul? To begin with the intellect. St. Thomas is willing to concede to the discarnate soul a measure of knowledge which is truly astonishing. The guiding principle which Aquinas follows is this: through death the soul of man becomes a spirit in the truest sense of the word, though it be the lowest degree of spirit; accordingly, let it be endowed with spirit activities, let it receive all that a spirit ought to possess. As insinuated already, this has nothing to do with the soul's sanctity or lack of sanctity; such intellectual enlargement would not even mean happiness unless other factors of the supernatural order come into play. The soul is naturally a spirit after death, be it for weal or woe. We cannot, of course, enter into details; St. Thomas is wise enough not to do so. We cannot give a description of that new intellectual life of the discarnate soul; all we can say is that it is a spirit, the lowest spirit, yet a spirit, and that it knows all those things which naturally belong to its sphere.

Volition of the disembodied human soul is a matter which is not without its terrors, for happiness and sanctity as well as their opposites ultimately depend on the state of man's will. Now though it is admitted by all theologians that the spirit, of whatever degree it be, has an unchangeable and an unchanging will, even scholastics are not united over the explanation of that unchangeableness, while they all admit it as a certain fact. Some say that it comes from God's withholding further graces; some think that the root of the unchangeableness lies in the very essence of the spirit-nature. A fact, however, which is certain and, as I said, terrifying, admits of no doubt: the discarnate human soul, like all other spirits, has its will fixed unalterably: it remains in the same loyalty which it had embraced at the end of life, whether this means God or self.

A point raised by Catholic thinkers has a further interest: are the discarnate human souls endowed with certain executive powers of acting, of doing, nay, even of moving, in the spirit-sense of moving? Those spirits whom we call angels or demons have certainly such powers. Some scholastics, like the Scotists, have no hesitation in admitting that the souls of the dead can do things as other spirits can do them. St. Thomas seems to hesitate, yet, even with him the matter admits of no doubt; a careful study of his works reveals the fact that he, too, grants powers of acting to the dead; he falls back on the universal principle that the human souls have become pure spirits and must possess spirit-life, however exiguous that spirit-life may be.

The disembodied human soul could hardly be called a human person, it is an imperfect person, as it is an incomplete substance; it has an innate fitness, which is called a natural desire, to be reunited with the body, for it is only in that dual state of sense and spirit that the human personality is entire and has its full range of activities. These considerations, which are the best which Catholic philosophy can offer, do not present a cheerful view of the world of the dead. Even independently of the possibility of actual reprobation, man's soul, separated from the body, outside the supernatural sphere, must be regarded as a maimed being, one that is deprived of the splendors of human life and human personality, for though our theologians grant spirit-activities, such powers are no real enjoyment to the souls that possess them. We are not surprised, therefore, to find that human tradition, outside the influences of the Christian revelation, has taken a gloomy view of the realm of the dead.

VII

The Intercourse of the Living with the Dead

It is one of the oldest beliefs of mankind that the living may, under certain circumstances, get into touch with the dead. This superstition, if we must give such a name to this belief, is at least an indirect evidence that men have always admitted in practice some kind of survival of the human personality after death. It would be difficult to describe with any accuracy the kind of existence that men have attributed to their dead, yet they have endowed them with substance and reality sufficient to make them agents of good and evil in practical life. In the oldest portions of the Scriptures, in Deuteronomy, we find this practice of holding intercourse with the dead condemned as one of the great sins among the doomed races of Canaan:

> Neither let there be found among you any one that shall expiate his son or daughter, making them to pass through the fire: or that consulteth soothsayers, or observeth dreams or omens. Neither let there be any wizard. Nor charmer, nor any one that consulteth pythonic

spirits, or fortune-tellers: or that seeketh the truth from
the dead. For the Lord abhorreth all these things: and for
these abominations he will destroy them at thy coming
(Deut 18:10-12).

The earliest instance of necromancy recorded in the Bible
is an attempt to consult one who was among the dead, as
to the future; Saul the king went to the woman that had a
divining spirit at Endor:

And he said to her: Divine to me by thy divining spirit,
and bring me up whom I shall tell thee." And the rest
of the story may be told in the full text, for the meth-
ods of necromancy have not altered in the course of the
centuries. "And the woman said to him: Whom shall
I bring up to thee? And he said, Bring me up Samuel.
And when the woman saw Samuel, she cried out with
a loud voice, and said to Saul: Why hast thou deceived
me? for thou art Saul. And the king said to her: Fear
not. What hast thou seen? And the woman said to Saul:
I saw gods ascending out of the earth. And he said to
her: What form is he of? And she said: An old man
cometh up; and he is covered with a mantle. And Saul
understood that it was Samuel, and he bowed himself
with his face to the ground, and adored. And Samuel
said to Saul: Why hast thou disturbed my rest that I
should be brought up? And Saul said: I am in great
distress; for the Philistines fight against me; and God is
departed from me; and would not hear me, neither by
the hand of prophets nor by dreams. Therefore have I
called thee, that thou mayest show me what I shall do.
And Samuel said: Why askest thou me, seeing the Lord
is departed from thee, and is gone over to thy rival? ...

And forthwith Saul fell all along on the ground, for he was frightened with the words of Samuel (1 Sam/1 Kings 28:11-16).

From this long narrative taken from the Book of Kings, we can gather what is meant by the expression in the older Biblical document, Deuteronomy, "to seek the truth from the dead." It is not merely some form of vain observance by which definite meanings would be attached to happenings concerned with the bodies of the dead; by the dead are meant the spirits who are not seen, but who are credited with knowledge, and who may, under given circumstances, impart that knowledge to the living. Shall we say *a priori* that this ancient belief of mankind is a complete deception, and that the dead are powerless to do anything either for or against man? Here, of course, I must remind the reader that I am concerned with this problem in its natural aspect only; the intercourse which the living may have with the holy dead, with the elect, the spirits of the just, is a different matter altogether, belonging to that great mystery, the Communion of saints; in that blessed sphere anything may happen in God's providence, the saints may appear to the living and teach and guide and help them on to eternal salvation. Our subject demands no such exceptional state; we are simply asking whether the spirits of the dead—in other words, the dead—have it in their power to influence the living. This question may be approached from three different points of view. Firstly, we may ask in an abstract manner whether any spirit can manifest himself to man. Secondly, we may inquire if that special class of spirit, the discarnate human soul, has it in his power so to do. The third point to be settled is of a general order; granted that spirits have such power, is it within God's providence to allow them to exercise the power? And here we must recognize the difference between the *absolute* and the *conditional* in the divine ordinances. In his omnipotence God may prevent spirits of every class from the exercise of such power, or he may permit them to exert it, even though its exercise would be against his commands, and would, in fact, be a sin on the part of the spirits.

There is such a bulk of tradition that spirits not only may exert influence over man but may actually manifest themselves to him, speaking with him in his own language, that it would be temerarious to refuse to the spirit-world this privilege of communicating with humanity. We take it for granted here that a spirit when he enters into converse with man does so under definite human forms which it is in his power to assume; it matters little to our purpose whether these forms are merely subjective impressions on man's senses or have some objective consistency. The saints of heaven have come and talked to their friends and clients here on earth, angels have appeared, and demons have been allowed to tempt Christ's disciples as they tempted the Master himself in the desert. Must we make an exception for the discarnate human soul in its natural state? There seems to be no *a priori* reason why we should do so; the separate human soul possesses spirit-qualities and it ought to be granted those powers which spirits ordinarily possess. We may, indeed, limit those powers to the least possible range compatible with a spirit-nature—after all, the discarnate soul is the lowest and weakest form of spirit—but to refuse it spirit-activities, spirit-motions, would be illogical. So I should not advise any antagonist of necromancy and spiritism to base his denunciations of that black craft on the powerlessness of spirits to do anything; it is just possible that such spirits might be able, and even might be allowed, to do much.

Thus this question is really one of divine ordinance. Does God allow such intercourse, in the sense that he does not inhibit, through some act of his providence, the activities of the discarnate, human spirits? We know, of course, that he does not prohibit the activities of demons absolutely, though he may limit and confine them, lest we perish. This is the intention of our daily prayer after Mass:

> Holy Michael, Archangel, defend us in the day of battle;
> be our safeguard against the wickedness and snares of
> the devil. May God rebuke him, we most humbly pray;
> and do thou, Prince of the heavenly host, by the power
> of God, thrust down to hell Satan and all wicked spirits,
> who wander through the world for the ruin of souls.

It is our constant cry to God to defend us against our spiritual enemies; we are given the armour of the Spirit that we may be able to withstand them. Does God restrict the evil human soul in its discarnate state in the same manner? I use the term "evil" here in connexion with the souls of the dead, because in this matter we are concerned only with such spirits as are neither in purgatory nor dwelling with Christ in heaven. On general theological and psychological principles it would be safe to assume that God deals with human spirits in the same way as with all other spirits; thus we may base on these foundations the same attitude which mankind has instinctively held for so many ages and ascribe to the dead real powers, we may give them initiative, we may without hesitation accept it as a possibility that certain human spirits may make their presence felt among the living, especially in those places which were the scenes of their human activities.

Thus our considerations are brought down to this very simple issue: whether or not it is lawful for man here on earth to attempt to enter into communication with the dead and, in the words of Deuteronomy, to seek truth from them. Now it is evident that the Catholic Church has never hesitated in her condemnation of every kind of spiritism; for her, spiritism is merely necromancy. I need not enter here into the phases of modern spiritism; the "seeking of truth from the dead" is one of the most serious wounds in our modern society. That strange things do happen at seances is a matter beyond doubt; it would be rash to treat it all as delusion or imposture. Orthodox writers differ in their interpretation of the origin of these alarming occurrences. Some say that the evil spirits, the demons, the fallen angels, are the dark powers that manifest themselves they seem to take it for granted that human souls could not in any way show such activities. But, as we have already said, there is not the least reason why discarnate human souls should not behave in the same way as demons. The principal conclusion at which we should arrive is this: that to whichever grade those spirits may belong which are responsible for the communications of the medium, they are not good but bad spirits; whether they be human or demoniac matters but little in the ultimate outcome.

This conclusion is, obviously, supremely abhorrent to the bulk of modern spiritists. They deny on principle that it is an evil thing to seek truth from the dead, and maintain, therefore, that if the dead answer, such behaviour, far from being blameworthy, shows love and interest on the other side. When the spiritist is reproached with the apparent futility, nay, even the nauseousness of many of the spirit-communications, his answer is that, if not all intercourse with the dead is above suspicion, there may be a kind of communication that has all the quality of a highly ethical act. If spirits are consulted by men of science and virtue concerning good and holy things, even with respect to religious issues, and if the spirits give reply worthy of a wise man, is not spiritism justified through the very decorum of its behaviour? I readily admit that a type of spiritism might be developed which would deceive even the very elect, and from which all coarse and vulgar elements could be eliminated, though it would not seem that hitherto spiritism has been anything but a degrading necromancy. I do not think that there is any other answer against spiritism when considered in all its possible aspects than this: God has proscribed it for man as he forbade man to partake of the tree of the knowledge of good and evil. This is the standpoint of the Catholic Church; and unless people are ready to accept this divine prohibition they are not unlikely to fall into the snares of the spiritists.

The following typical case, under the pseudonym of Titius, was propounded to the Holy See: Titius, banishing from his mind every intention of holding intercourse with evil spirits, is in the habit of calling up the spirits of the dead. He behaves as follows: finding himself alone, without any preliminary, he prays to the chief of the heavenly army that from him he may obtain power to enter into touch with the spirit of a given person. He waits a little, holding his hand ready to write, and all at once he feels that his hand is moved; thus he knows that the spirit is present. He asks what he wants to know and his hand writes the answers to his queries; these replies invariably squaring with the Catholic faith and the Church's doctrine concerning eternal life. As a rule they have to do with the state in which the soul of some dead person finds itself; they speak of the necessity of prayers for the dead and also complain of the ingratitude of relatives and so on. Is this manner of acting lawful on the part of Titius?

The answer of the Holy See was clear. Such behaviour is not lawful.

Again in 1917 with equal definiteness the Holy Office gave a complete denial as to the legitimacy of the practices described thus: Whether it be lawful to be present at any kind of spiritistic locutions or manifestations, questioning souls or spirits, listening to their answers, or even looking on, although there might be a tacit or express stipulation that there was no intention whatever to enter into any sort of cooperation with evil spirits. From the nature of the case such transgressions would be grievously culpable, as they would be sins against a grave precept of religion. So far the Church has not attached any kind of censure or excommunication to spiritistic practices, but she considers them to be mortal sin.

VIII

THE JUDGE OF
THE LIVING AND THE DEAD

No attribute is more constantly predicated of God than judgement. With the boldness of a friend, Abraham appeals to God and reminds him of this supreme quality when interceding for the men of Sodom:

> Far be it from thee to do this thing, and to slay the just with the wicked, and for the just to be in like case as the wicked. This is not beseeming thee: thou who judgest all the earth, wilt not make this judgement (Gen 18:25).

It would be a big volume that would be written were all the utterances of the canonical writers concerning God in his capacity as Judge to be gathered together. By God's judicial power we mean something very definite and clearly discernible from other divine operations; we mean a constant intervention of God in the affairs of the created universe, arranging and rearranging both spiritual and material issues on account of the free actions of his rational creatures. Though judgement is more obviously associated with God's punitive interference it is not, of course, confined to the divine severities; the most adorable portions of his judgements are those providential mutations in the course of the universe which are the rewards of the virtuous actions of the children of God.

There is, however, one important fact to be borne in mind, that right through the Old Testament God is represented as exercising the supreme function of Judge, not in the distant future only, but in the immediate present, with men, with nations living now on this earth. The prophets who announced the great Judgement were not speaking of an event to take place in a future world, but of severities and rigours to be shown by God towards the living generations of men. God's function of Judge is, in Scriptural thought, essentially a continuous function, an unceasing function, not one that is reserved exclusively for a special date hereafter. I do not say that there are not very clear allusions by the prophets to a judgement at the end of times, but the bulk of their vaticination is of judgements to be executed within a short space of time. Thus Isaiah uses language which goes far beyond the threats against Egypt or Babylon or Tyre:

> With breaking shall the earth be broken, with crushing shall the earth be shaken as a drunken man, and shall be removed as the tent of one night. And the iniquity thereof shall be heavy upon it: and it shall fall and not rise again (Isa 24:19-20).

If we come to the New Testament, to the Person of the Incarnate God, we find that he likewise is endowed with the power of judging, with the power of separating good and evil, of awarding to men their due, according to their deserts, long before the hour of final judgement. It is in the New Testament that the expression occurs "Judge of the living and the dead." This name for God is not found in the Old Testament, and in the New Testament it is given invariably to the Person of Christ:

> He commanded us to preach to the people and to testify that it is he who was appointed by God, to be a judge of the living and the dead (Acts 10:42).

How are we to understand this extension of God's judicial power to the dead? Does it mean that God has not judged men in their lifetime to the full extent, so that he completes after death the judgement of men? Or shall we see in this formula only a drastic expression of the all-embracing power of divine justice, from which nothing can escape? It is indeed not easy to see the full meaning of this inspired phrase. As every generation of living men will soon belong to the world of the dead, it is not apparent who are the living in contradistinction to the dead whom God is said to judge. Doubtless, the simplest interpretation is this: that as God deals with men and nations on this earth according to the dictates of his justice, so he will dispose of them in that other state, the state of death, giving to each man his due. By the formula "Judge of the living and the dead" is meant, I think, not always a twofold classification of human beings, but the complete career of the same beings, their conditions of life and death, whose happenings, whose details, are equally in the scales of divine justice. This phrase, used by St Peter and St Paul, has also been inserted in the oldest symbols of the faith: "He shall come again with glory to judge the living and the dead." As the Creed identifies Christ's judgement of the living and the dead with his second Coming, it may be said that, in this instance at least, by the living are meant those human beings who shall be found alive on this earth at his advent, while the dead are those who will come forth from their tombs. But as we have seen in a former chapter, it is New Testament language to give Christ a general dominion over the living and the dead in a kind of universal visualizing of the whole human race:

> For to this end Christ died and rose again: that he might
> be Lord both of the dead and of the living (Rom 14:9).

We may now come to the interesting point how the various judgements which are attributed to the supreme Judge of the living and the dead are to be distinguished from each other and yet correlated; for Christ, even as is the Father, is always seated on the throne of judgement.

The distinction I submit in order to proceed clearly in this vast subject is as follows: we must recognize God's *temporal* judgements and also his *eternal* judgements. The discrimination between the temporal and eternal judgements is a most far-reaching doctrine in this matter: the decrees of the temporal judgement have a concluding point, while those of the eternal judgement are endless in effect. Again, both of these distinctions contain a sub-distinction: God's temporal judgements are concerned with men either in their bodily state on earth or in their disembodied state; his eternal judgements deal either with individual men or with the whole race. So we have four aspects of the great doctrine of God, the Judge of the living and the dead. Men, either individually or as races or nations, as families or even as religious bodies, receive rewards or punishments while they are on earth. Or again, if the divine justice in its temporal equalization of conditions is not satisfied, there is that other adjustment which goes by the comprehensive name of purgatory, and which all theologians agree in describing as a portion of the temporal punishment for sin.

At death the soul of man is definitely fixed either in election or reprobation, its eternal fate is sealed, it is said to be condemned by God's justice or to be admitted into the society of the elect, also by God's justice, though theologians, with edifying humility, generally prefer to say that the soul is granted entrance to everlasting life through the mercy of God. This portion of the eternal judgement is hidden and affects, so to speak, the very substance of man's individual personality. To it is given by all theologians the name of particular or private judgement. This denomination we may keep here, provided we remember that even in the first class of judgements—the temporal judgements—there is also something very particular and private to the individual, such, for instance, as the punishment due to each soul in purgatory for its own sin. The judgement of a man who dies in mortal sin ought to be called the particular eternal judgement, in contradistinction to the particular temporal judgement which is the lot of one dying in a state of grace, who yet has to undergo temporal punishment.

Then there is finally the Last Judgement, the results of which will also be eternal, but which will be concerned essentially with the whole human race, in soul and body, with the greatest possible manifestation of all hidden things. It is pre-eminently the Day of Judgement, the one great act of God as the supreme Judge of the living and the dead. In the following chapters we shall give a fuller account of these four divisions of God's judicial activities; at present I am trying to make clear to the reader the connexion of the different spheres of the divine justice; for it is evident that, radically speaking, there is only one judgement, and the four acts constitute one mighty drama of God's sanctity. Theologians constantly warn us that there are never new judgements, but that the one judgement is progressive till it reaches consummation on the Last Day.

This, then, is that divine march of him who, in the words of Abraham, "judges all the earth." The temporal administration of divine justice has this one great object, to vindicate God's sanctity even in the case of those who will ultimately be saved, because they, too, have offended much against his justice; even the saints are punished here on earth lest the anger of God destroy their chances of salvation; the elect are punished after death in the avenging flames of the purgatorial state because, though they be saved, they are saved out of many sins "as through fire." The grave judgements of God here on earth have, moreover, a power of grace for man, that man by them should be converted and live, that he should be warned and frightened when he hears the blows of the divine judgements. The writings of the Fathers are full of that *leit motif;* they seem to have understood the judgements of God in their temporal aspect more clearly than we do. So we may say that God's temporal judgements in this life and after death have an essentially providential character in the sense that they are meant as chances of ultimate salvation; they are temporal, because the punitive arrangements of which they consist will end sooner or later. The human being to whom the judgements of God have been, to the very end of his life, a useless lesson will be judged finally at death as one incapable of eternal life, because he did not want to understand the judgements of divine justice. It may be said, with full theological accuracy, that man is judged and condemned eternally because he despised God's temporal judgements.

The relation of the Last Judgement—the fourth act—to these preceding ones has been a favourite theme with the Fathers and theologians of all ages. Why will there be that great, that universal Assize, when it is apparent that the justice of God has never been idle, in fact, seems to have had its full scope; when all those who are unworthy of eternal life are already condemned, when God has punished man, has brought things back to the golden rule of justice with his unceasing severities towards men in their days of life and even after death, in purgatory? The most satisfying view and the one that seems to have the support of reiterated scriptural language is this: that the Last Judgement is truly the manifestation of all the judicial acts of God that have gone

before; there is no new judgement, but there is the proc-
lamation to all flesh of the complete justice of God in all
previous judgements. For the three previous judgements are
mostly hidden, are incomprehensible to man, they cannot
be followed by the eye of man, they are too complex to be
understood by man. Now it is the special function of the
Last Judgement to make clear before all creation that not
one evil thing has remained unvisited, not one good thing
has passed unrewarded, in all the vast history of the human
race:

> Every man's work shall be manifest. For the day of the
> Lord shall declare it, because it shall be revealed in fire.
> And the fire shall try every man's work, of what sort it is
> (1 Cor 3:13).

St. Thomas gives expression to this thought in a very
lucid fashion: there are two operations in God; the first,
the creation of all things; the second, the government of
all things. Both these operations have as their complement
a judgement. To the operation of creation corresponds the
Last Judgement, while the other set of judgements are con-
gruous to the operation of government; and this for very
clear reasons:

> Through the judgement which corresponds to the gov-
> ernment of the world—which could not be carried out
> without judgement—everyone is judged individually
> for his works, not only as far as it concerns himself, but
> also as far as it concerns the government of the world.
> For this reason the reward of one man is delayed for

the benefit of other people, and the punishment of one becomes the benefit of another. For this reason it is necessary that there should be another universal judgement which is the direct counterpart of the first creation of all things; so that, in the same way as all things then came forth from God without an intermediary, so there will be a final finishing off of the world, everyone receiving ultimately what is due to him according to his own personality. Therefore in that judgement divine justice will show itself manifestly in all those things which are now hidden, for this very reason that one man is sometimes so treated as to be of utility to other men, a treatment contrary to that which his well-known works seem to merit. For this reason, too, there will then be the most extensive separation between the good and the bad, for there will be no longer room for that arrangement by which evil men are helped by good men and good men are helped by bad men; for as long as the present state of life is under the government of divine providence there is this mixing together of the good and the evil for their mutual benefit (*Suppl.* q. 47, a. 1).

IX

The Temporal Judgement

We may now consider the various judgements in themselves, and we may watch Christ at his great work as Judge of the living and the dead. As all judgement has been given to him, we shall use indiscriminately the name of God and the name of Christ in connexion with judgement for the remainder of our book.

The temporal judgements are indeed a most important province of Christ's activities in his judicial capacity; if we left them out of our theology the whole matter of God's judgements would become distorted and even incomprehensible. As already insinuated, by temporal judgements we mean those ordinances of Christ, be they punitive, be they remunerative, which take place in time, outside eternity. We do not say, of course, that their results will not go beyond time, will have no eternal repercussions; everything God does is meant in some way to have effects that modify man's everlasting destinies. The distinction between eternal judgements and temporal judgements is to be found in the arrangements of divine providence, of which some are transient, some are permanent. Thus, for instance, if through a just judgement of God a Christian prince were to lose his temporal powers, for, say, not being loyal to the Church, this would be a temporal judgement, since the loss of power would not necessarily affect the eternal fate of the prince's soul; the punitive arrangement is not, in such a case, an immutable state, affecting eternity itself.

Christ, since he ascended to heaven and took up his position at the right hand of the Father, is most certainly acting as the Judge of mankind. Judgement is more than providence, or better still, it is the moral side of providence. The free deeds of men and above all of Christians, their prayers, their virtues, their sins, are matters which the divine Judge contemplates unceasingly, and he orders all things in perfect equity. This is the meaning of St Paul's splendid words to the Corinthians:

> For he must reign, until he hath put all his enemies under his feet. ... And when all things shall be subdued unto him, then the Son also himself shall be subject unto him that put all things under him, that God may be all in all (1 Cor 15:25-28).

The coming of Christ is itself described as a judgement. That separation between good and evil which is the purpose of all judgement, begins with the Incarnation:

> And Simeon blessed them and said to Mary his mother: Behold, this child is set for the fall and for the resurrection of many in Israel and for a sign which shall be contradicted (Luke 2:34).

But the separation was not then manifest, it only began to become visible, at least relatively, after the Ascension, when there took place in such terrible and evident fashion the casting away of that people who had rejected the Son of God. Christ's Redemption on the Cross is the greatest act of divine judgement. He was then struggling beneath the burden of all the injustice committed by man against the Father, he was judged by God as though he bore the guilt of all sins, and by his acceptance of that suffering and that death in his own flesh he made complete payment of the debts of his brethren to divine Majesty:

> Blotting out the handwriting of the decree that was against us, which was contrary to us. And he hath taken the same out of the way, fastening it to the cross (Col 2:14).

So we hear Christ saying confidently a few days before his Passion:

> Now is the judgement of the world: now shall the prince of this world be cast out (John 9:31).

And again Christ says that the Spirit will convince the world of judgement "because the prince of this world is already judged" (Luke 17:11). The Baptist had made the same announcement in a metaphor of unmatched power:

> He shall baptize you with the Holy Ghost and with fire: Whose fan is in his hand: and he will purge his floor and will gather the wheat into his barn: but the chaff he will burn with unquenchable fire (John 3:16-17).

The temporal judgement of Christ is concerned with spiritual punitions and rewards as well as with temporal ones; for let us bear in mind that divine judgements are exercised over that most important possession of man, his graces, as well as over his external goods:

> And Jesus said: For judgement I am come into this I world: that they who see not may see; and they I who see may become blind (John 9:39).

The temporal severities are announced when Christ speaks of what is manifestly the end of the Jewish people as his "day," for by "day" is here meant judgement:

> Even thus shall it be in the day when the Son of man shall be revealed. In that hour, he that shall be on the housetop, and his goods in the house, let him not go down to take them away: and he that shall be in the field, in like manner, let him not turn back. Remember Lot's wife (Luke 17:30-32).

It is true that several times our Lord says that he came, not to judge the world but to save it:

> God sent not his Son into the world, to judge the world: but that the world may be saved by him (John 3:17).

How are we to reconcile these apparently contradictory utterances? The explanation seems to be a simple one, namely that during the days of his mortality, before his exaltation, Christ did not, as Man, exert his judicial power, at least in the external government of the world. Thus it is in the same sense that he says he was only sent to the lost sheep of the house of Israel, though we know he was sent to the whole human race. But after Christ's Ascension Christians never hesitated to attribute to him the vastest activities as Judge of the world; they looked to him for the redress of their grievances when they suffered at the hands of persecutors; they confidently believed that the pagan world, above all, pagan Rome, would soon feel the heavy arm of the divine Judge:

> Therefore shall her plagues come in one day, death and mourning and famine. And she shall be burnt with the fire: because God is strong, who shall judge her. ... Rejoice over her, thou heaven and ye holy apostles and prophets. For God hath judged your judgement upon her (Rev 18:8, 20).

> True and just are his judgements, who hath judged the great harlot which corrupted the earth with her fornication and hath revenged the blood of his servants at her hands (Rev 19:2).

Christ himself is seen coming out of heaven by the prophet of Patmos at a period of human history which does not appear to correspond with the end of the world:

> And I saw heaven opened: and behold a white horse. And he that sat upon him was called faithful and true: and with justice doth he judge and fight (Rev 19:11).

This is the true view of Christ; this makes him into a living power. Genuine Christian sentiment has ever been deeply impregnated with this trait of Christ as the just Judge, and Christians have always found it possible to love him with the tenderest love because they know him to be such; they speak to Christ with all the familiarity with which Abraham spoke to the Lord his friend, when he praised his justice as they overlooked the cities of Sodom and Gomorrha. Our Jesus would be less amiable if he were less true and less powerful in his judgements.

The doctrine of the divine judgements is stated very often in other terms, such as the doctrine of temporal punishment for sin; but it is in truth one and the same thing. Christ punishes man with temporal punishments because he executes judgement over man. The doctrine of temporal punishment says that man owes the divine justice satisfaction, and even great satisfaction, after the stain of sin has been taken away from his soul by the grace of God. The punishment is meted out by God's providence, either in this life or in purgatory.

In no province of sacred theology are we so much in need of the fundamental doctrine of Christ's judicial power, for the sake of clearness, as in the case of the Church's teaching on purgatory. It seems difficult to give any other explanation why so many amongst the saved must pass through the purgatorial state than the truth so simply expressed in the old Catholic phrase that the souls of men have to pay a debt to divine justice. A more superficial view of purgatory would be this: that the souls of men pass into the other life ignorant, with the stains upon them of many venial sins and the impediments of innumerable imperfections. We exclude, of course, the state of mortal sin, as such a state is tantamount to eternal reprobation. We might call this view of purgatory the psychological view, as it implies that the process of purgatorial purification would be a gradual transition of man's disembodied spirit from a lower to a higher grade of power. But such a view seems excluded by another very important consideration: the souls in purgatory are pure spirits. Now spirits operate at all times with the entirety of their being. So theologians have to admit that the moment the saved soul enters into the spirit-state it turns to God with a completeness of surrender which is not comprehensible to man here on earth, and which establishes it in perfect charity. So the purgatorial process ought to be taken in an exclusively juridical sense.

The word *purgare* in Latin law means "to pay the full amount of the punishment due." So our best theologians in speaking of purgatory use the language of the law courts; the divine Judge decides, assesses, the amount of penalty to be undergone for offences and neglects not fully repaired during mortal life. What those pains and penalties are, we need not investigate here; they belong to another portion of theology. But it seems evident that nothing can account for the burdens thus put on those holy spirits except the direct act of the divine Judge; nor could a finite authority settle how much or how little of penalty each such spirit must undergo.

> Be at agreement with thy adversary betimes, whilst thou art in the way with him: lest perhaps the adversary deliver thee to the judge, and the judge deliver thee to the officer, and thou be cast into prison. Amen I say to thee, thou shalt not go out from thence till thou repay the last farthing (Matt 5:25-26).

The purgatorial adjustment of the divine claims might almost be called an afterthought in God's providence, because the general plan of salvation which God has produced for man is such that if man were faithful he would reach the hour of death in a state of perfect justice, having done his day's work, and having produced for his Master that amount of profit which his Lord has a right to expect from him.

The Church's liturgy is full of invocations to God and his Christ that man may find mercy with his Judge. These prayers, which are so profoundly Christian, refer, of course, to the temporal judgement, for the eternal judgement is unalterable. When we hope to be judged leniently we expect Christ to relinquish in our favor some of his rights as Judge, either in this life or in purgatory. It is in connexion with this judgement also .that we have those solemn promises of Christ that according to the mercifulness of our own judgements, judgement shall be shown to us:

> Be ye therefore merciful, as your Father also is merciful. Judge not: and you shall not be judged. Condemn not: and you shall not be condemned. Forgive: and you shall be forgiven. Give: and it shall be given to you: good measure and pressed down and shaken together and running over shall they give into your bosom. For with the same measure that you shall mete withal, it shall be measured to you again (Luke 6:36-38).

X

THE ETERNAL JUDGEMENT OF INDIVIDUAL SOULS

The designation of "particular judgement" has been applied for a long time now as a kind of technical term to that act of God by which the soul of man at death is either received into the society of the elect or is rejected and cast away forever. The main features of the particular judgement thus understood are its peremptoriness and its complete secrecy. Of no human being do we know with certainty that he has been rejected by God, though, on the other hand, we do know of definite human beings having been admitted into the society of the elect, as, for instance, all the canonized saints. But no eye has seen what really happens between God and the human soul at that first moment when the soul finds itself in eternity. Though this name "particular judgement" more commonly brings home to us the idea of possible reprobation of individual souls, such a one-sided aspect of this act of God would leave in obscurity the most marvellous manifestation of the divine sanctity and justice. For the elect, for those who are saved, that moment which constitutes the soul in eternity is an overwhelming revelation of God's fidelity; not only does it become immensely clear to the soul that it is saved, that it is in a state of grace, that it belongs to God for ever and ever, but all the works done in the supernatural order during the mortal life are remembered by God, are brought to the knowledge of the fortunate soul, are seen in their full setting; and God rewards as only God can reward.

> For I know whom I have believed and I am certain that he is able to keep that which I have committed unto him, against that day (2 Tim 1:12).

Or again:

> I have fought a good fight: I have finished my course: I have kept the faith. As to the rest, there is laid up for me a crown of justice which the Lord the just judge will render to me in that day: and not only to me, but to them also that love his coming (2 Tim 4:7-8).

In the case of the elect there is this double marvel of divine justice and truth: they are given, firstly, that eternal life which they have always sought, and secondly they are also granted that additional glory which comes from every fresh merit. The inspired writers seem to have been particularly struck by God's fidelity in remembering all the works of the elect. It is divine judgement in its most glorious and most consoling form; it is justice superabounding, because not a cup of cold water given in the name of Christ will be without its reward. The good works of the elect follow their entry into eternity like a cortege of angels:

And I heard a voice from heaven, saying to me: Write:
Blessed are the dead who die in the Lord. From henceforth now, saith the Spirit, that they may rest from their
labours. For their works follow I them (Rev 14:13).

Though for many of the elect the bestowal of that reward may
perhaps be delayed through the captivity of purgatory, still
their immense treasure of merits is for ever secure, the justice
of God will not allow him to let anything go unremunerated.
Merit and reward belong to another part of theology; here we
look upon them as the pronouncement of a judgement. In
their essential quality they will be bestowed on the discarnate
human soul when it is admitted into heaven; when it will
be granted not only the blessed Vision of God but various
degrees in that Vision. May we not say, speaking now naively,
that the greatest surprise of the elect at that blessed moment
will be to find how God has remembered even the least of
their deeds; how their works, long forgotten by themselves,
are truly recorded in the Book of Life?

Theologians have gone deeply into the matter of that
"finding" of all the merits of a long life at the first moment
of eternity. They would love to construct theories which
would account for the presence of all that past merit in
the soul; they say, for instance, that grace has never ceased
growing as merit grew, so that the soul at death has already
the full wealth of spiritual beauty, though in a hidden way.
However, with the ups and downs of human life, and very
often with long interruptions of mortal sin, it seems difficult
to explain completely how all the works of the elect revive
when they enter heaven, unless we admit God's own power

of restoring to man all his past merits.

The term "to judge" has, in New Testament language, generally the unfavourable sense of judgement for condemnation, though the word "judge" as substantive stands for God in his office, both as rewarder of merit and avenger of sin. So our Lord says:

> He that believeth not in him (Christ) is not judged. But he that doth not believe is already judged: because he believeth not in the name of the only begotten Son of God. And this is the judgement: Because the light is come into the world and men loved darkness rather than the light. For their works were evil (John 3:18-19).

With this divine utterance we approach the dreadful subject of man's condemnation to eternal reprobation after death. In reprobation, as in election, there are two elements which must be kept apart in our consideration of the subject: man is admitted into the society of the elect because he dies in the state of grace, but he also receives a higher or lower degree of eternal life according as his merits are great or small. So, on the other hand, man is cast into eternal death because temporal death found him in a state of mortal sin, but his degree of punishment will depend on the amount of evil which he did in life and which had not been forgiven. In very exact theology we should say that man is admitted to eternal life or is cast away, not by a judgement that takes place over him after the separation of the soul from the body, but by that judgement through which God decided that death should overtake the holy one in a state of grace, whilst, through the permissive will of the divine justice, death was allowed to come to the sinner when he was in the state of mortal sin. Theologians would not be unwilling to say that there is no real pronouncement of sentence, either of eternal life or of eternal death, these great issues following naturally, as it were, from the state of the soul at the moment of death. In this matter we have our Lord's own words in the verse quoted above: "He that believeth in him is not judged. But he that doth not believe is already judged: because he believeth not in the name of the Son of God. And this is the judgement...." But we may, of course, take the less technical view and say that souls are condemned or are exalted by a just judgement of God when they enter eternity. We certainly cannot get away from a definite act of God which settles for ever man's fate by putting an end to the period of mutability and change.

There is, however, in the case of the reprobate as well as in the case of the elect, the great question how God deals with individual guilt, because he cannot treat alike, even in reprobation, the great criminal and the ordinary sinner. The fact of reprobation itself, of being cast for ever into exterior darkness, is a necessary result of final unrepentance, of the state of mortal sin at death. Between reprobation thus considered as a deprivation of eternal life, and the just punishment to be inflicted for the great human sins, there must, of course, be a very grave difference. How this difference makes itself felt in the lost spirits of all degrees of guilt it is not possible for us to say. We have no clear guidance on this subject. We know definitely what constitutes the higher or the lower degree of reward among the saved: it is always a deeper comprehension of God in his Essence. More and more of divine life is added unto the soul. With the lost we have no such provision. So we may content ourselves with the general principle that sin is visited in eternity according to its gravity. The *Inferno* of Dante is the poetical presentment of a very grave truth. Yet it is good Christian feeling to hold that the vindictive justice of God is not as comprehensive as is his remunerative justice; even the reprobate is punished less severely than he deserves. One theological principle whose validity is beyond doubt could be invoked here to bring out this difference in remuneration and punishment. Whatever supernatural merits man had during lifetime, those merits are counted unto him as an increase of glory, though it may have happened very often that by the act of mortal sin the merits were, so to speak, killed. If the sin is repented of, if the Christian die in a state of grace, all his merits are revived for him. Now there is no such bringing back of past sin. So, if a man has sinned much but has repented, even if afterwards he sin again and die in his sin, those sins are not brought back to him of which he had repented.

The profoundest things said by any theologian in this matter of eternal reprobation is the utterance of St. Thomas Aquinas:

> Eternity of pain does not correspond to the gravity of the guilt but it corresponds to the irreparable nature of the guilt (*Summa* I-II q. 87, a. 5).

It may seem strange at first sight that a less guilty man should be lost everlastingly as much as one who may be a million times more guilty. Now according to St. Thomas the real punishment inflicted by divine justice does not lie in the fact that it is everlasting, for such everlastingness is the condition of everything spiritual, but that the special burden lain on the reprobate spirit corresponding to his guilt is indeed the direct act of the divine judgement. What this punishment is we have no means of knowing. But as Catholic theology has always maintained that reprobation is entirely the result of divine justice, this doctrine has its mitigations in its very definition. We do not say of any man that he is eternally subject to this or to that torment; in such a case we should find it difficult to give an explanation that would be satisfying. But we say that God visits justly all sins for which there is not due repentance before death. So to speak, we approach the whole subject from God's point of view, and we leave it with God; we know he could do nothing unjust without denying himself.

XI

THE LAST JUDGEMENT

The phraseology of the Scriptures does not always make it very apparent whether certain happenings which are prophesied are to be catastrophic events of short duration or long periods of God's visitation. Thus, in the various utterances, of Christ concerning the end of the world it is not easy to distinguish lengthy times of tribulation from sudden manifestations of God's anger, appearing with the rapidity of lightning. Many of God's judgements are long drawn-out punitions and the catastrophic chastisements are, on the whole, rare. A thought frequently expressed in a certain class of modern literature is this, that the World's History is the World's Judgement. There is much truth in such a view. There is, however, no doubt whatever concerning the nature of the Last Judgement; it is described as an event of terrifying suddenness and as something entirely outside the historic development of mankind. Its date is so mysterious that no one knows it, not even the angels of God:

> But of that day and hour no one knoweth: no, not the angels of heaven, but the Father alone (Matt 24:36).

Even the signs which are to be the precursors of that day will be no clear indication of its exact hour:

> For yourselves know perfectly that the day of the Lord shall so come as a thief in the night. For when they shall say: Peace and security; then shall sudden destruction come upon them, as the pains upon her that is with child. And they shall not escape (1 Thess 5:2-3).

The last Judgement, therefore, ought to be regarded by us as a great mystery, both as to its date, as to its nature, and as to its purpose.

We can, in a way, understand the meaning of those temporal judgements of which we have spoken above; we can even grasp the doctrine of God's dealings with the soul at death; but when we come to the Last Judgement we are in presence of a dogma which is entirely outside all experience and for which we have no terms of comparison. Very wisely, in a passage quoted in a former chapter, St. Thomas considers the Last Judgement as the counterpart of the creation of all things out of nothing. No finite measure can be applied to that greatest of all events, it is an act on an infinite scale. It is true that several very precious hints are dropped by the inspired writers as to its tremendous import, but the few suggestions which are given are in themselves allusions to possibilities quite beyond our grasp. The most constantly recurring idea is this, that God will reveal all things on that day; but it is easy to see that such revelation is a mystery, great beyond all words. So we must exert our faith and believe that God will make all things manifest, as we believe that at the beginning he created light. How this revelation will take place no finite mind can know, because it is truly the revelation of an infinite thing—the whole economy of God's grace on the one hand, and the whole range of the created free will on the other; so that not only facts but even possibilities will be disclosed, in order to discover to every eye God's providence in all its perfection.

Nor would it be in keeping with Catholic thought to say that the Last Judgement is nothing else than the beginning of eternity or the state of eternity. It is to be an event, a passing act of finite duration, not an everlasting condition. There will be a moment when that great judgement will begin and there will be a moment when it will end, though its results will be interminable. In other words, it will be an act of God such as he never did before and such as he will not again repeat. Never again will the human race be gathered in all its entirety as at that supreme hour, but that such an assemblage of all the human beings that ever existed will take place is one of the very few clear indications concerning that act of God that has been made known, though the race, thus brought together, will be separated again, and this for all eternity:

> And when the Son of man shall come in his majesty, and all the angels with him, then shall he sit on the seat of his majesty. And all nations shall be gathered together before him: and he shall separate them one from another, as the shepherd separateth the sheep from the goats: And he shall set the sheep on his right hand, but the goats on his left (Matt 25:31-33).

A revelation will then be made which will be truly miraculous in its effects, but transient as a divine act. This revelation will be given to the wicked as much as to the elect. It is a manifestation of God's justice and sanctity, different in kind from that Vision of God which the elect in their souls enjoy even now before the great day. Nothing but an act of divine omnipotence can explain that manifestation of God's justice to all flesh. This great event is invariably called the "day of the Lord" as if it were an event so particularly different from all other historic happenings as to be the one day outside eternity worthy of the Son of God. Its importance will be commensurate with the Person of the God Incarnate.

The day of the Lord consists in four manifestations of God's omnipotence whose literal reality cannot be doubted by any Catholic: there will be the destruction of the physical world through fire; there will be the raising up of all the dead; there will be the revelation of all the hidden things of man's conscience and God's providence; and then, ultimately, there will be the separation of the good and the wicked. The day of the Lord will contain all that, and the term "Last Judgement" may be applied to this whole complex of divine operation. It is certain that the Resurrection of the dead will precede the Judgement, properly so-called; there is more room for doubting the sequence of happenings with regard to the universal conflagration, but it would seem that the fire in which all men then living will find their death will be the first act in this tremendous drama. Out of the ruins of the world that was till then, a new world will be created which will be truly part of the Resurrection. It will be in that new world that the

Judgement will take place; it will be in that new world that Christ will appear in glory and majesty. St. Thomas adopts this order for these great mysteries. The world will be purified in that searching fire and the reprobate will be cast out of it, because they will be unworthy of it in its new perfection.

It is evident that no pictorial presentment can be attempted of so vast a change of all things. The great ideas of the Scriptures are still the most potent and most satisfying expressions. To try to depict the Last Judgement will always be a miserable failure, even if the artist be a Michael Angelo. Just let us take in their literal meaning words like the following, in which the four great facts are described, and we shall be as near visualizing that solemn truth as it is possible for man to be.

> The Lord delayeth not his promise, as some imagine, but dealeth patiently for your sake, not willing that any should perish, but that all should return to penance. But the day of the Lord shall come as a thief, in which the heavens shall pass away with great violence and the elements shall be melted with heat and the earth and the works which are in it shall be burnt up. Seeing then that all these things are to be dissolved, what manner of people ought you to be in holy conversation and godliness? Looking for and hasting unto the coming of the day of the Lord, by which the heavens being on fire shall be dissolved and the elements shall melt with the burning heat. But we look for new heavens and a new earth according to his promises, in which justice dwelleth (2 Pet 3:9-13).

Wonder not at this: for the hour cometh, wherein all that are in the graves shall hear the voice of the Son of God.

And they that have done good things shall come forth unto the resurrection of life, but they that have done evil, unto the resurrection of judgement (John 5:28, 29).

> Their conscience bearing witness to them: and their thoughts between themselves accusing or also defending one another. In the day when God shall judge the secrets of men by Jesus Christ (Rom 2:15-16).

> Then shall the king say to them that shall be on his right hand: Come, ye blessed of my Father, possess you the kingdom prepared for you from the foundation of the world... Then shall he say to them also that shall be on his left hand: Depart from me, you cursed, into everlasting fire, which was prepared for the devil and his angels (Matt 25:34, 41).

Christ will do the judgement in Person, he will appear as the God-Man, in full glory. Whether his coming will be before or after the conflagration and the Resurrection it is not possible to say; but that he will execute judgement is in the very essence of our Creed: *Qui venturus est judicare vivos et mortuos.* Much more, indeed, could be said concerning the many speculations of theologians about things of such magnitude; but there is just one article of St. Thomas which, through its very dignity, is not out of place here: "Whether the judgement be done by word of mouth":

> It is difficult to say with any certainty what is true in this matter; however, it seems more probable that all that judgement from the point of view of the discussion, from the point of view of the accusation of the wicked, and of the praise of the good, and from the point of view

of the sentence pronounced over both classes, will be carried out only mentally. For if the deeds of every one were spoken orally, a length of time would be necessary, great beyond all concept (*Suppl.* q. 88, a. 2).

There are in the Gospels and in the Epistles words of great solemnity which compel us to stop one moment more in our considerations on the Last Judgement. Christ and his Apostles declare, with the greatest emphasis possible, that the elect will also judge, that they will be seated in majesty as judges on that day:

> And Jesus said to them: Amen, I say to you that you, who have followed me, in the regeneration when the Son of man shall sit on the seat of his majesty, you also shall sit on twelve seats judging the twelve tribes of Israel (Matt 19:28).

St Paul makes use of this great Christian hope in order to pour contempt on the quarrelsomeness of some of the Corinthians who went to law before the unbelievers:

> Know you not that the saints shall judge this world? And if the world shall be judged by you, are you unworthy to judge the smallest matters? Know you not that we shall judge angels? How much more things of this world (1 Cor 6:2-4)?

Such words are too clear to admit of any other interpretation than a literal one. There will evidently be an active participation of the elect, or at least some of the elect, in that final condemnation of the world. The Fathers freely use a term which no doubt recalled a familiar scene in the Roman law courts, they speak of assessors, men who sat by the side of the judge, by their very presence giving support and approval to his verdict; it was natural for them to say that the saints will be Christ's assessors on that day. The practice of religious poverty in life or the merit of martyrdom would single out a person to be specially fit to be Christ's assessor when he will speak his terrific anathema over sinful mankind. But even without metaphors it ought to be easy for us in a way to understand that the very contrast between the high sanctity of so many of the elect and the darkness of the reprobate will be a judgement severe beyond words.

We could not conclude this chapter without reference to a matter which is one of the undying controversies of both friend and foe. The enemies of Christ's Godhead have often said—and they are still saying it—that Jesus had what might be called an eschatological obsession; he was under the impression that the world would soon come to an end, and he announced his appearance as Judge of the living and the dead as an event not far distant, in fact to take place in the lifetime of the men who were his foes. And as such a catastrophe has evidently not taken place, Christ's claim to be God is an untenable ambition. On this subject volumes have been written. It is certain that our Lord warned the men with whom he lived, and especially the Apostles, always to watch lest their Lord and Master, coming at an unexpected moment, find them asleep. But, on the other hand, it is just as evident that Christ leaves the hour of that advent in great uncertainty and that no

one could conclude from his words that he taught a coming in the immediate future. There is in all those passages
which either inculcate vigilance or else leave the date of the
Master's return in such uncertainty, a blending of the near
future and the mysteriously remote future which is truly unparalleled. Thus, speaking of the near future, Christ
says:

> Take ye heed, watch and pray. For ye know not when
> the time is. Even as a man who, going into a far country,
> left his house and gave authority to his servants over ev-
> ery work and commanded the porter to watch. Watch ye
> therefore (for you know not when the lord of the house
> cometh, at even, or at midnight, or at the cock-crowing,
> or in the morning): Lest coming on a sudden, he find
> you sleeping. And what I say to you I say to all: Watch
> (Mark 13:33-37).

All this sounds as if Christ meant his Apostles to expect the
possibility of the Judgement at any time, and yet in the verse
before: "But of that day or hour no man knoweth, neither
the angels in heaven, nor the Son, but the Father" (Mark
13:32), we have his most emphatic utterance as to the un-
knowable character of the great event.

So we have again a description on the part of our Lord
of the kingdom of God which is anything but catastrophic:

> And he said: So is the kingdom of God, as if a man
> should cast seed into the earth, And should sleep and
> rise, night and day, and the seed should spring and grow
> up whilst he knoweth not. For the earth of itself bringeth
> forth fruit, first the blade, then the ear, afterwards the

full corn in the ear. And when the fruit is brought forth,
immediately he putteth in the sickle, because the harvest
is come (Mark 4:26-29).

Here we see the world's history described in the metaphor
of a ripening field: the Sower himself, who is evidently
Christ, is as one who leaves the seed to itself to do its work,
as one who has gone away. So we might multiply instances
of that mysterious blending of the two ideas, the necessity of watchfulness and the remoteness of the final har-
vesting. But if we bear in mind what has been said in an
earlier chapter, how Christ's judicial operations are unceasing, we can readily understand how there is need for every
man to be always on the watch. The coming of Christ to
each one at death is a complete judgement, and he who is
not prepared for that coming is truly a foolish man. Thus
those well-known parables on the necessity of watchfulness have been applied by the Christian doctors both to
the individual human being, always in danger of death,
and also to the whole human race, always in danger of the
catastrophic advent of Christ. This is truly a divine grasp
of the situation; what is true of man in his universality is
also true of man individually. If we take it for granted that
Christ at no moment ceases to be Judge, then we shall easily comprehend the complete actuality of all his parables
and utterances with regard to the imprudence of being un-
prepared for his coming. It is a terrible thing to fall into
the hands of the living God. Even without waiting for that
new world we serve him now with "fear and reverence. For
our God is a consuming fire" (Heb 12:28-29).

Whatever may have been the thoughts of the Apostles before Pentecost concerning the establishment of a triumphant kingdom of their Master during their own lifetime, it is certain that when once they had begun their great ministry the catastrophic coming of Christ was as much part of their preaching as it had been in that of their Lord. It was a certainty; the date of it mattered but little for practical behaviour, Christians had always to be ready:

> But the heavens and the earth which are now, by the same word are kept in store, reserved unto fire against the day of judgement and perdition of the ungodly men. But of this one thing be not ignorant, my beloved, that one day with the Lord is as a thousand years, and a thousand years as one day. The Lord delayeth not his promise, as some imagine, but dealeth patiently for your sake, not willing that any should perish, but that all should return to penance. But the day of the Lord cometh as a thief, in which the heavens shall pass away with great violence and the elements shall be melted with heat and the earth and the works which are in it shall be, burnt up (2 Pet 3:7-10).

Another form of illusion in this great matter of Christ's second advent has been much more universal, much more persistent, and is, in a way, more easily forgivable. This form of religious dreaming is even older than the Gospels; it is man's hope of the millennium. It has always been the faith of certain pious people, whom the iniquities of the world have afflicted in their souls, that there would be on this earth some day a very magnificent kingdom of God.

With the advent of Christianity it was, of course, Christ who would be the King of that happy era of human sanctity. It is not easy to contradict people and prove them to be wrong if they profess a hope in some mighty triumph of Christ here on earth before the final consummation of all things. Such an occurrence is not excluded, is not impossible, it is not at all certain that there may not be a prolonged period of triumphant Christianity before the end. The point of division between the legitimate aspirations of devout souls and the aberrations of false millenarism is this: the Chiliasts—as believers in the millennium are called, from the Greek word for thousand—seem to expect a coming of Christ and a presence of him in glory and majesty on this earth which would not be the consummation of all things but would still be a portion of the history of mankind. This is not consonant with Catholic dogma. The coming of Christ in the second Advent—the *Parousia*, as it is called technically—in orthodox Christianity is the consummation of all things, the end of human history. If before that final end there is to be a period, more or less prolonged, of triumphant sanctity, such a result will be brought about, not by the apparition of the Person of Christ in Majesty but by the operation of those powers of sanctification which are now at work, the Holy Ghost and the Sacraments of the Church.

The Chiliasts of all times and shades of opinion, and there are many to be found even to-day, seem to despair, not only of the world, but even of that dispensation of grace which was inaugurated at Pentecost; they expect from the visible presence of Christ a complete conversion of the world, as if such a happy result could not be otherwise brought about. They have still to learn the meaning of Christ's words to the Apostles:

> It is expedient to you that I go, For if I go not, the Paraclete will not come to you: but if I go, I will send him to you (John 16:17).

The Catholic Church has full confidence in the present order of supernatural life, and if she sighs for the return of her Christ it is not because she despairs of the work he has done, but because she desires to see that work made manifest to all men, that it may appear what wondrous things Christ accomplished for man before his Ascension into heaven.

CPSIA information can be obtained
at www.ICGtesting.com
Printed in the USA
LVHW081520210720
661230LV00028B/1369